The Joy of Chopin

Selected and edited by Denes A

This volume contains some of Chopin's most popular and technically most accessible works, ranging from intermediate to advanced grades. The selections, based on authentic texts, are presented in an approximate order of difficulty and, as such, can serve as an introduction to the fascinating world of the Chopin *oeuvre*.

Frederic Chopin (1810-1849) was born in Poland but spent most of his adult life in Paris, where he was, together with Franz Liszt, the center and idol of the artistic and literary world, both as a composer and as a virtuoso. He wrote for the piano exclusively and sublimely and became the poet laureate of that instrument early in his career to remain unchallenged to this day. His music is unique in many respects. The smallest section of a work of his, a sentence, a phrase, bears the unmistakable stamp of his stylistic individuality. This is a rare phenomenon in the literature of music. Even the greatest of masters, a Bach, or a Mozart, for instance, is not always readily identifiable from a musical fragment; Chopin always is.

Such striking individuality, of course, deserves and calls for a specifically knowledgeable and emotionally attuned approach on the part of the performer; a sensitive, rich, singing tone; elegant, well-articulated melody-playing; tasteful, excess-free *rubato* tempo; a keyboard touch that can be utterly delicate or passionately forceful; and last, but not least, judicious, well-planned use of the pedal. Performing Chopin's music must reflect its exquisite spontaneity and originality, which is at the core of its undiminished appeal and of the joy it affords for both the player and listener.

Order No. YK20998

Exclusive Distributors:
Hal Leonard
7777 West Bluemound Road, Milwaukee, WI 53213
Email: info@halleonard.com

Hal Leonard Europe Limited
42 Wigmore Street Maryleborne, London, WIU 2 RN
Email: info@halleonardeurope.com

Hal Leonard Australia Pty. Ltd.
4 Lentara Court Cheltenham, Victoria, 9132 Australia
Email: info@halleonard.com.au

Printed in EU.

Yorktown Music Press
New York/London/Sydney

CONTENTS

Mazurka
(1832)

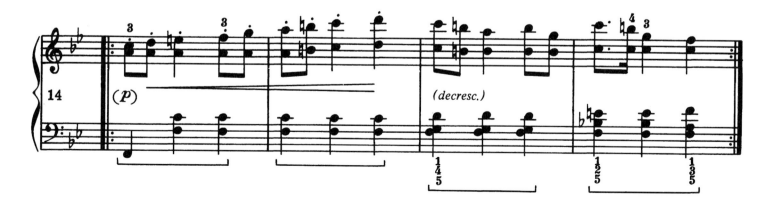

Ped. simile

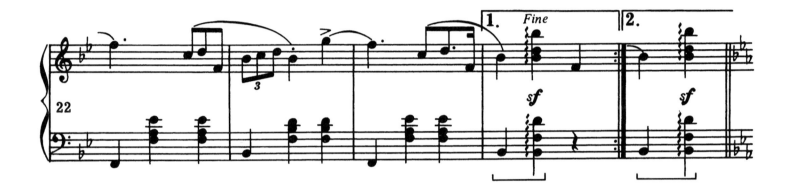

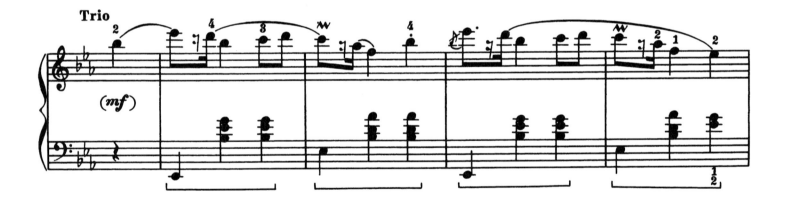

Trio

Dal segno 𝄋 al Fine

Valse
(Posthumus)

Con moto rubato

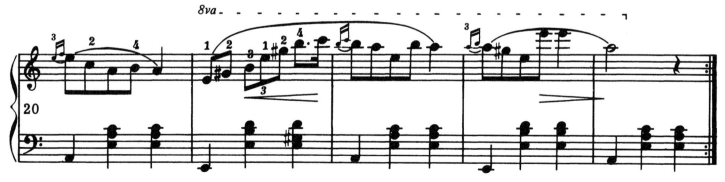

Nocturne
(Posthumus)

Lento con gran espressione

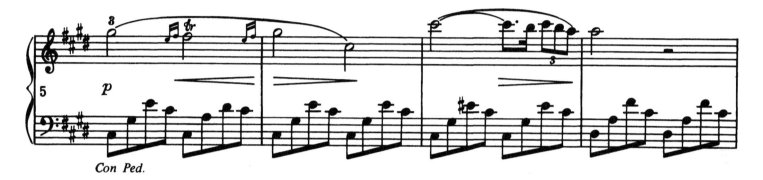

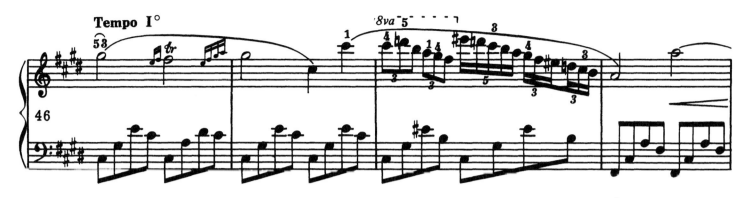

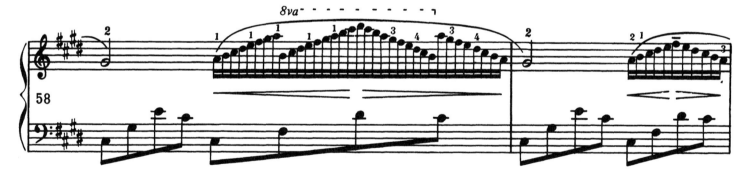

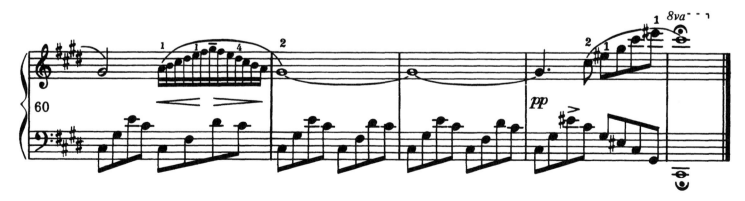

Mazurka
Op. 67, No. 3

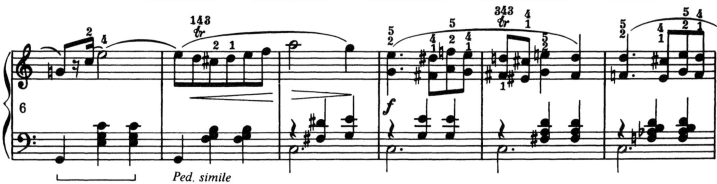

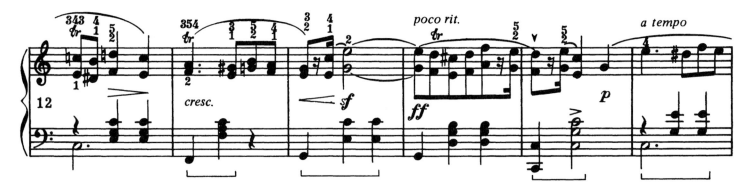

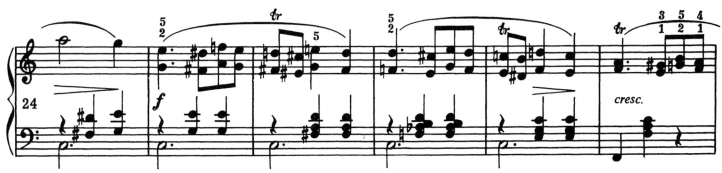

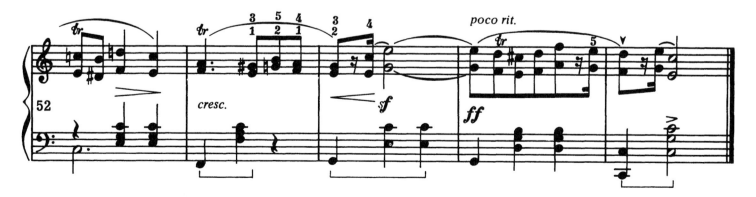

Prelude

Op. 28, No. 6

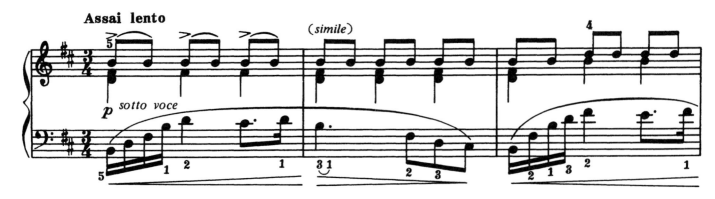

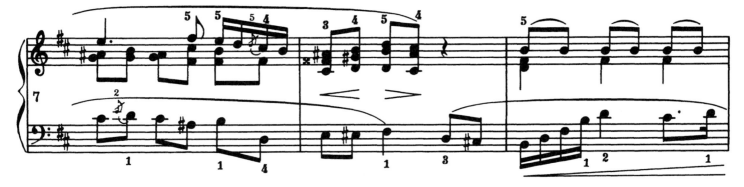

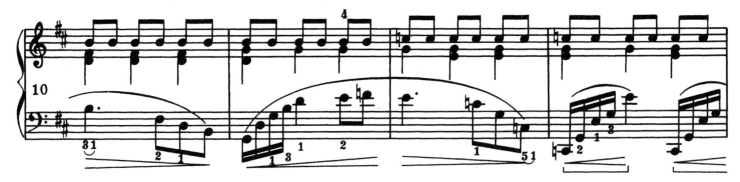

Prelude

Op. 28, No. 7

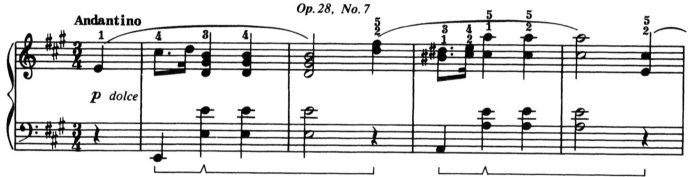

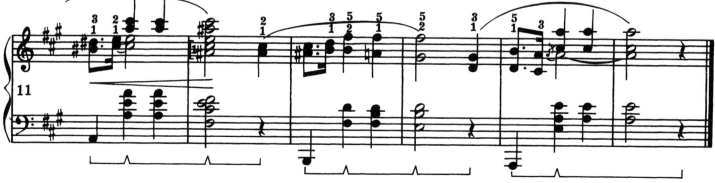

Nocturne
Op. 15, No. 3

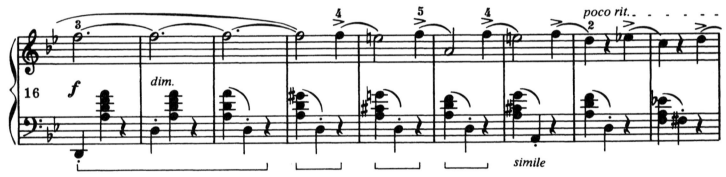

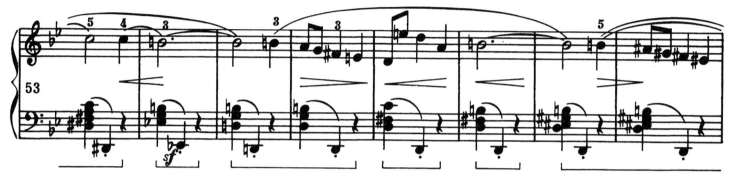

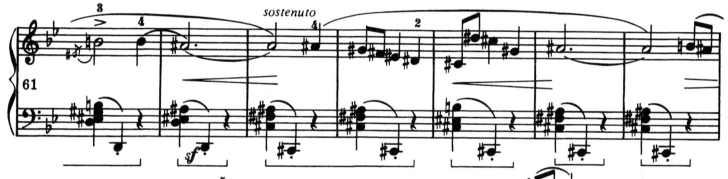

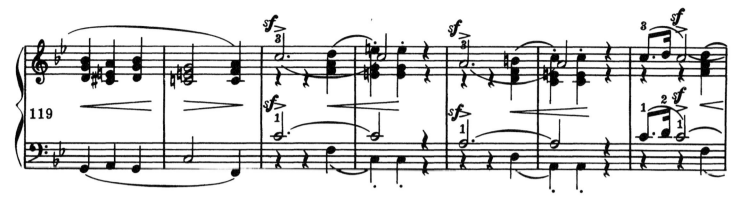

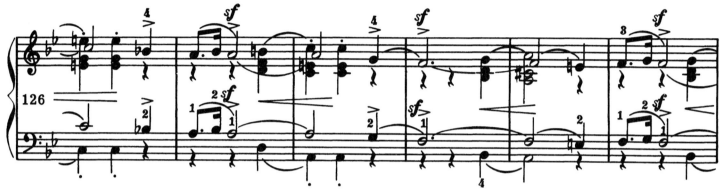

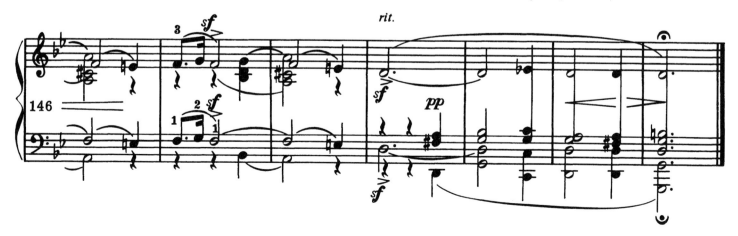

Prelude

Op. 28, No. 4

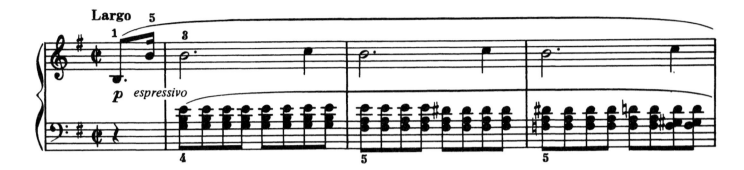

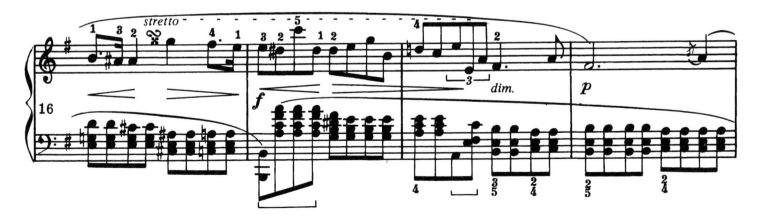

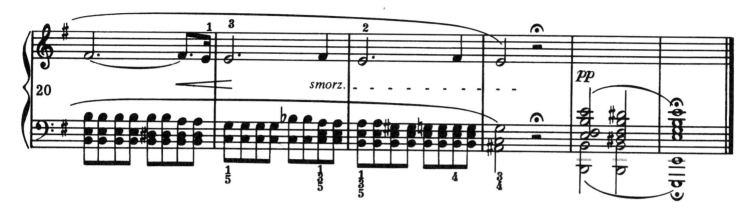

Prelude

Op. 28, No. 20

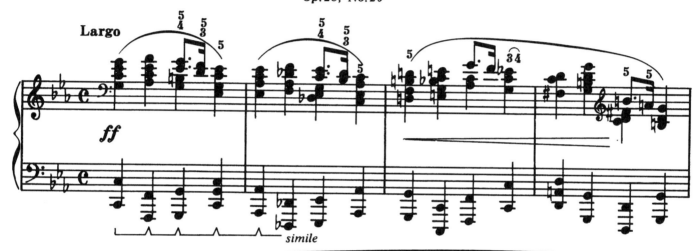

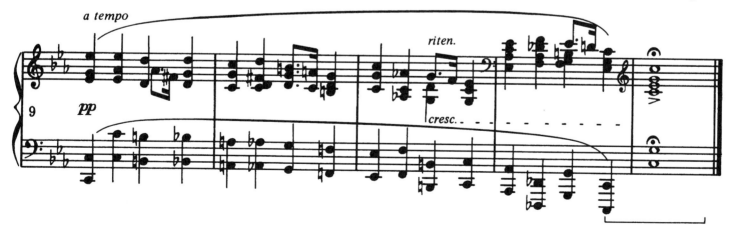

Mazurka
Op. 33, No. 1

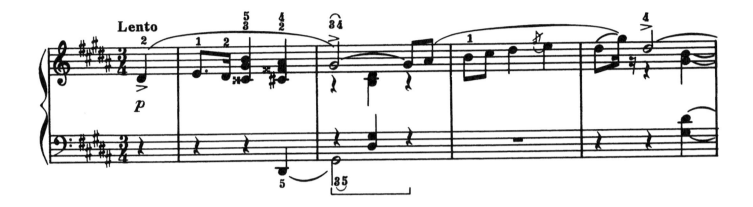

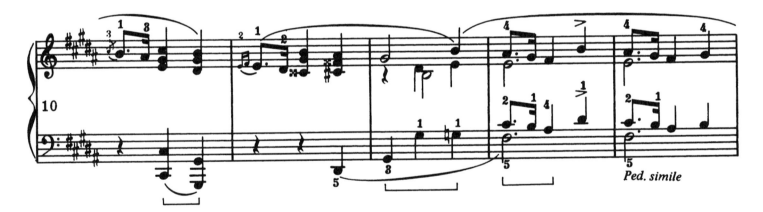

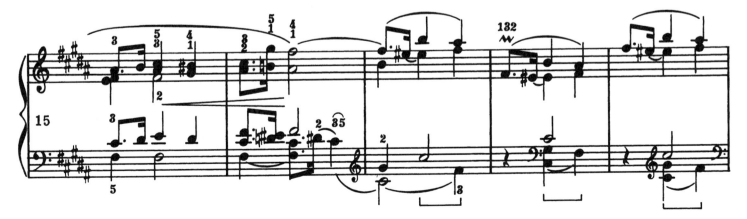

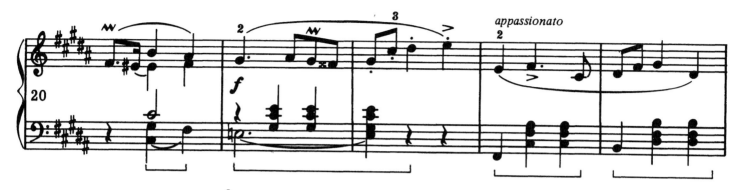

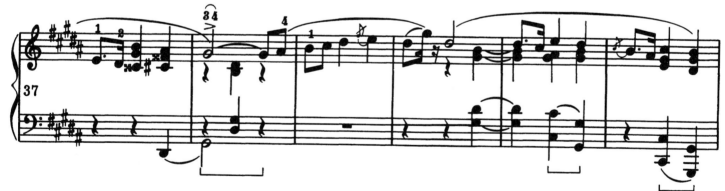

Prelude

Op. 28, No. 15

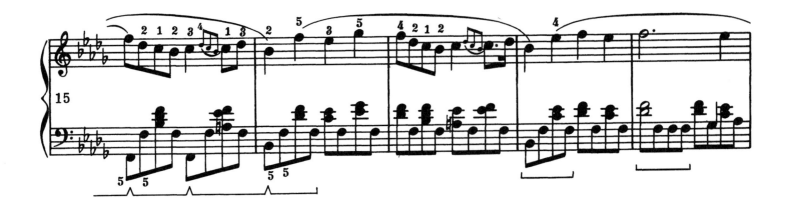

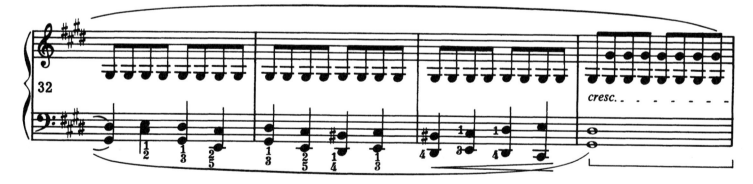

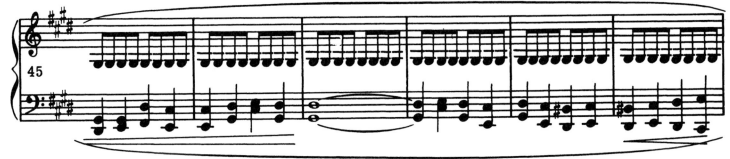

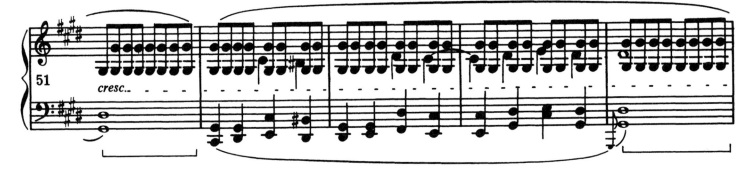

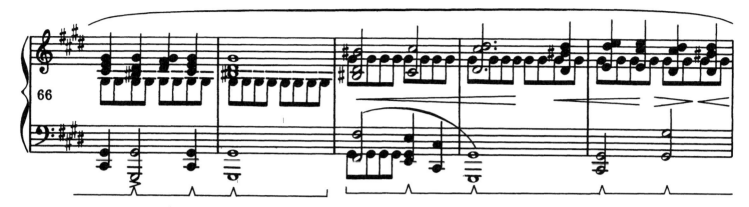

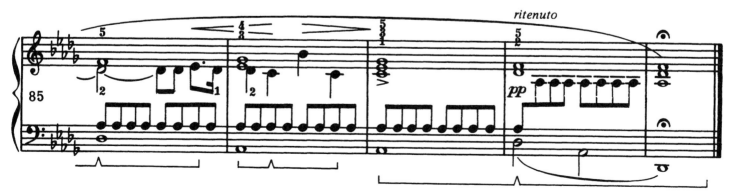

Mazurka
Op. 17, No. 4

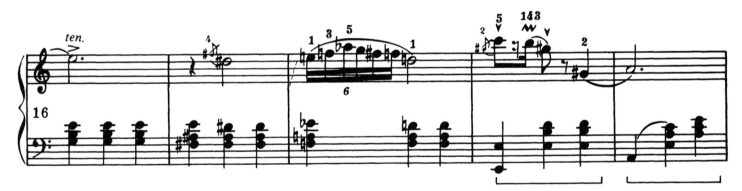

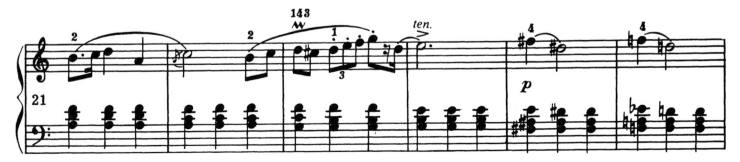

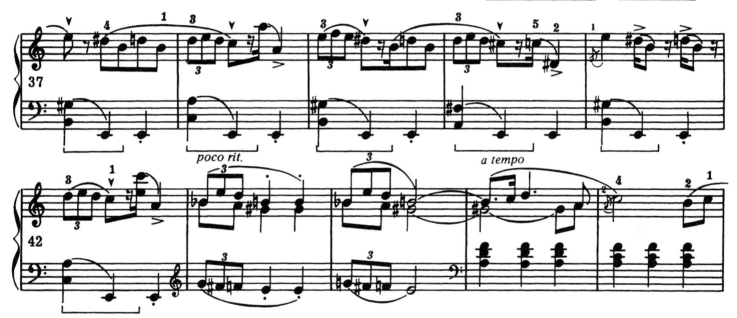

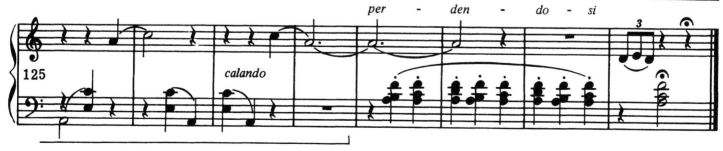

Valse

Op. 70, No. 2

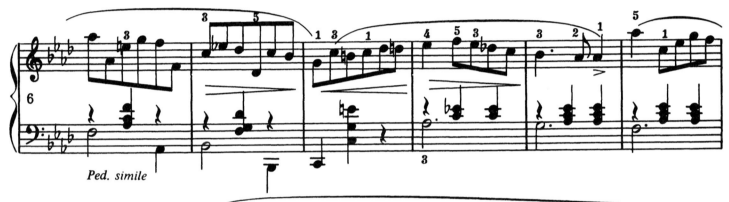

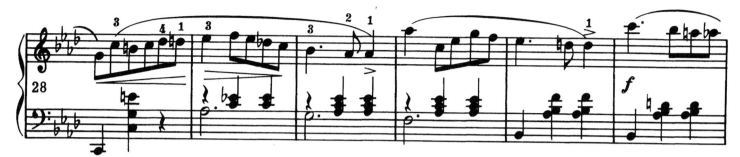

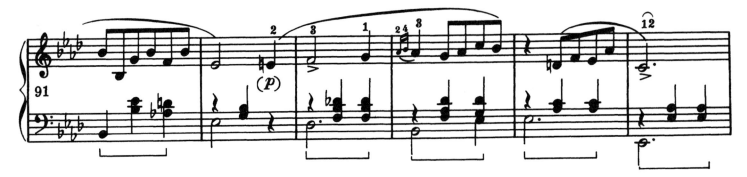

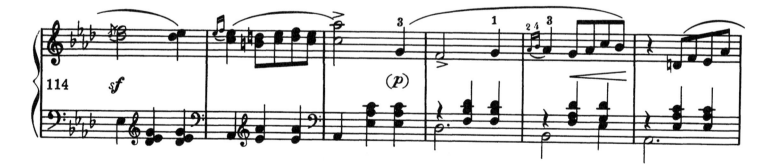

Valse

Op. 69, No. 2

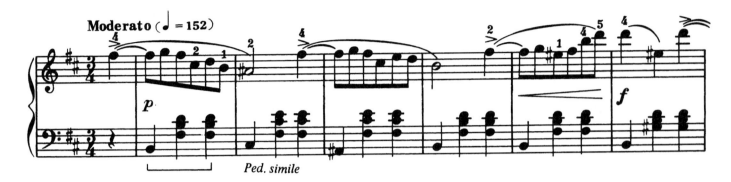

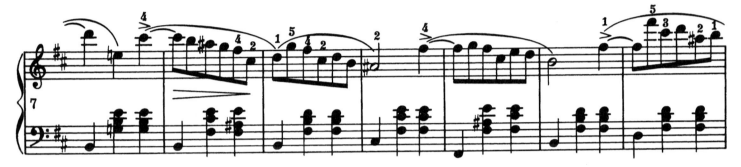

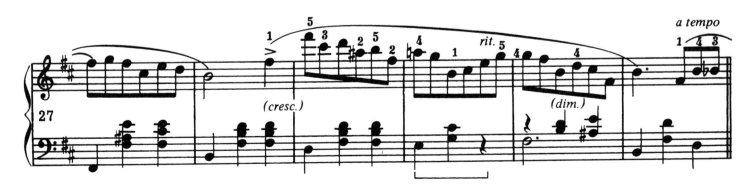

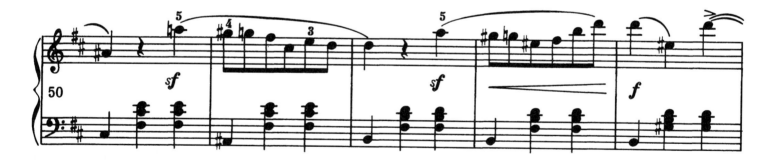

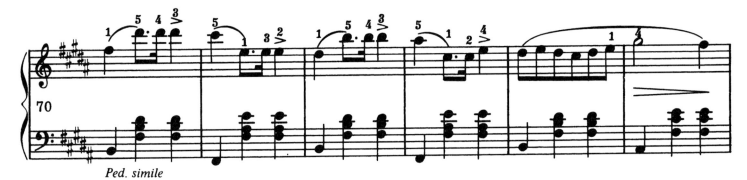

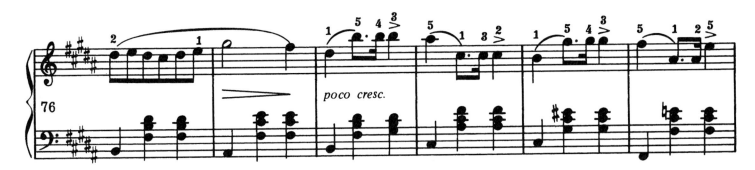

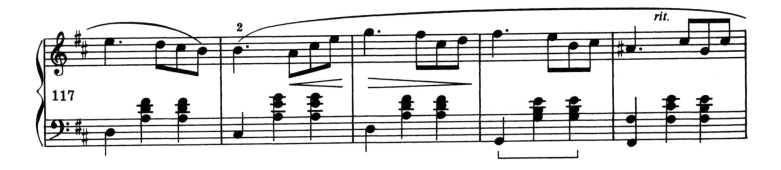

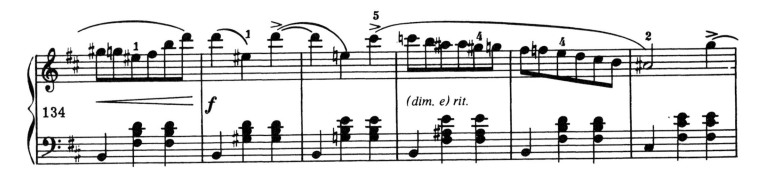

Three Ecossaises

Op. 72

1.

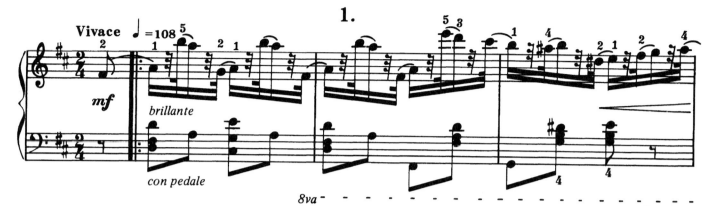

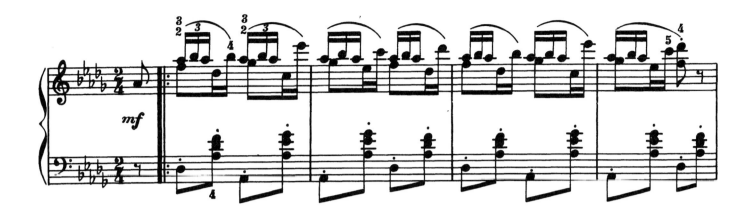

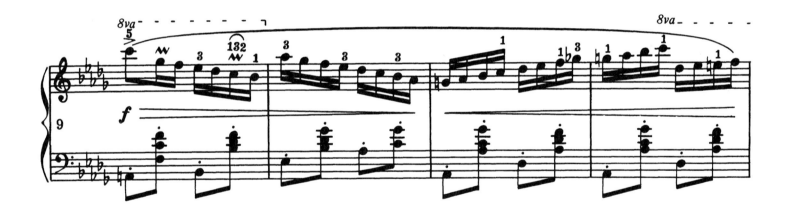

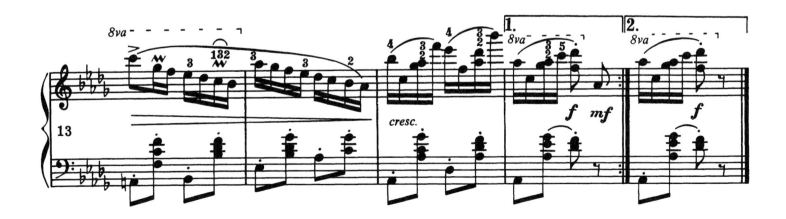

Etude

Op. 10, No. 3

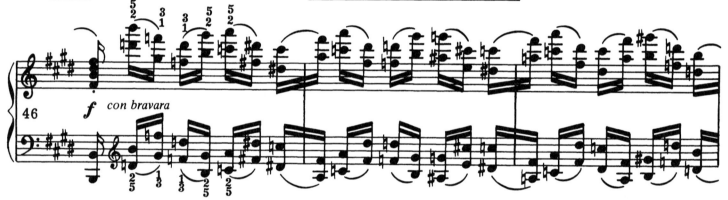

Funeral March

from Sonata No. 2, Op. 35

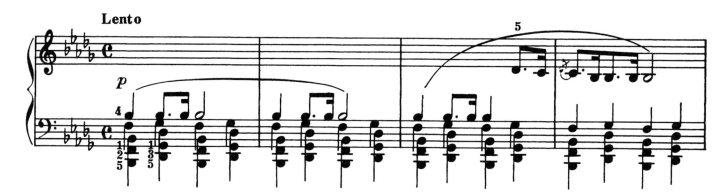

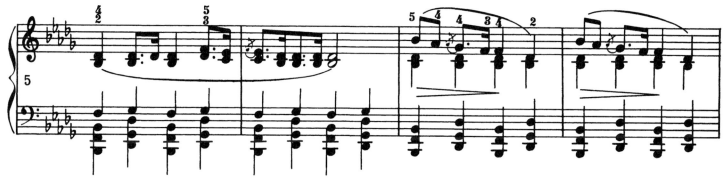

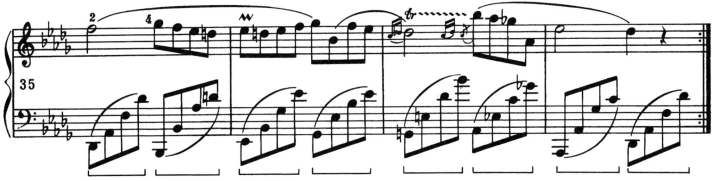

Etude

Op. 25, No. 7

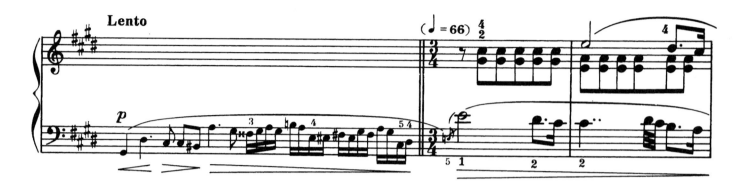

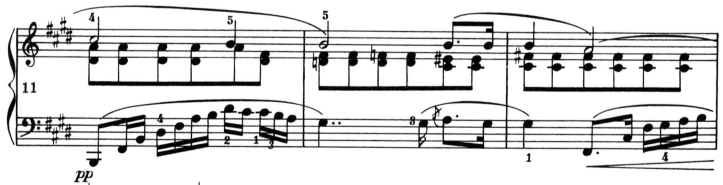

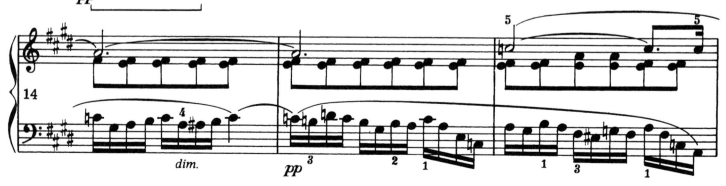

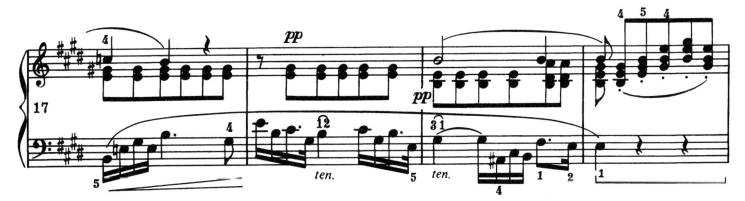

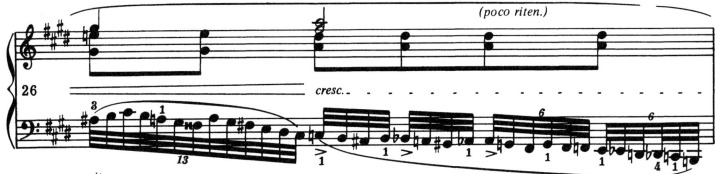

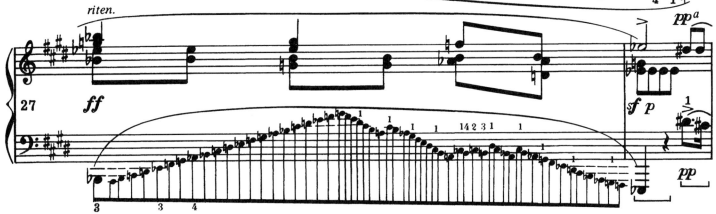

Valse

Op. 64, No. 2

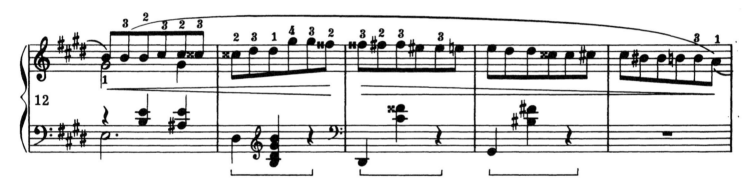

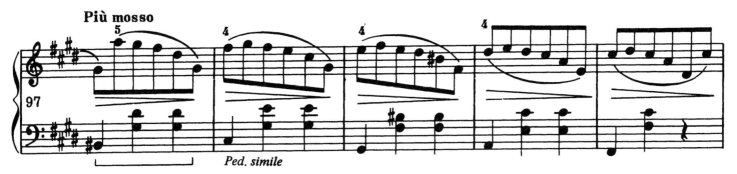

Tempo I

Polonaise
Adieu! An Wilhelm Kolberg

(Posthumus)

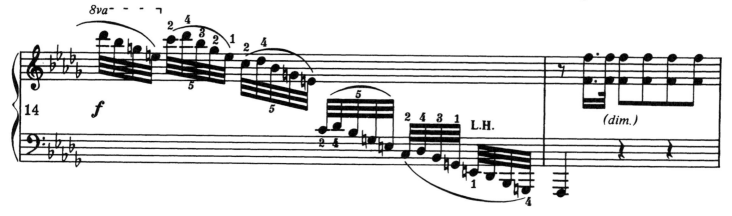

Fine

Trio

Auf Wiedersehen! *

pp con espress. Ped.

cresc.

(mf)

8va

(p) *(mf)*

* Based on an aria from Rossini's "La Gazza Ladra"

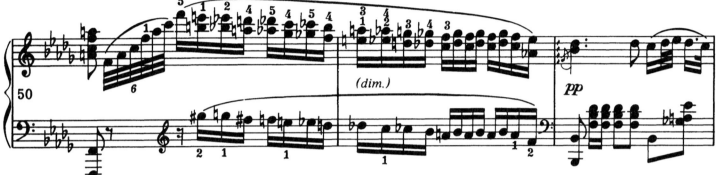

Polonaise da capo al Fine.

Etude
Op. 10, No. 5

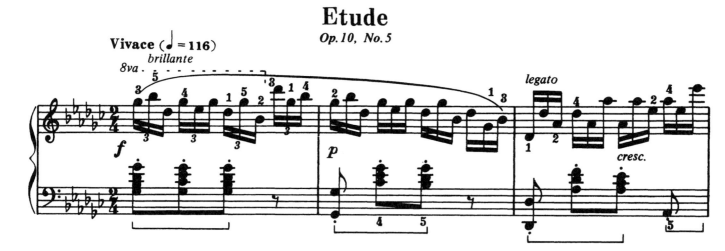

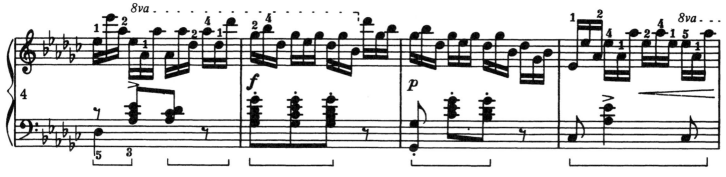

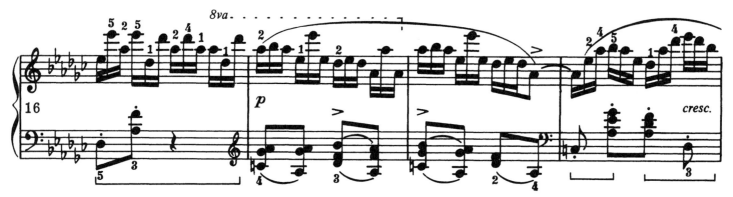

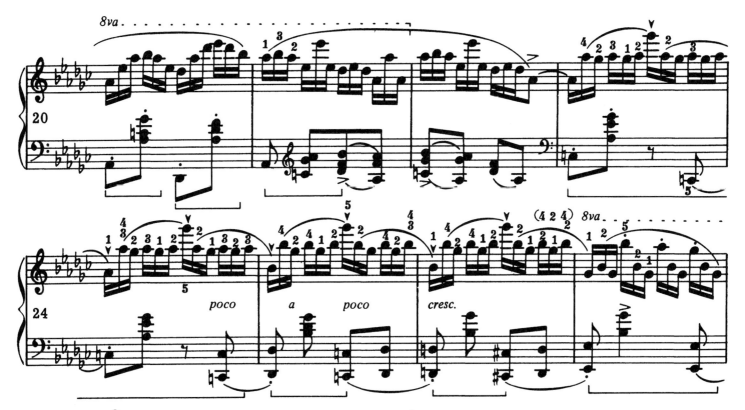

Polonaise

Op. 40, No. 1

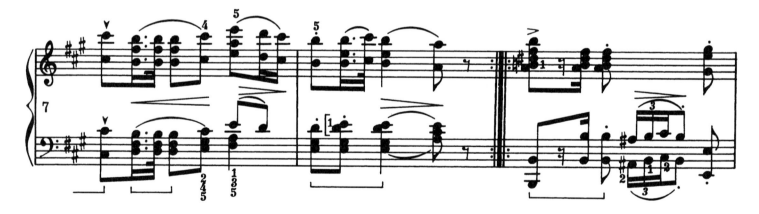

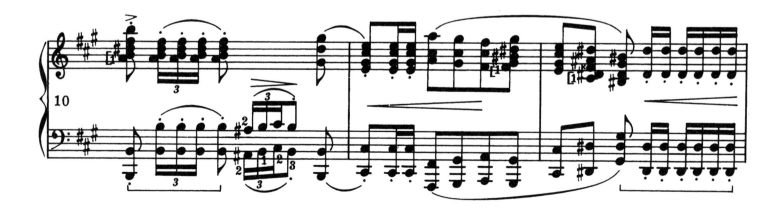

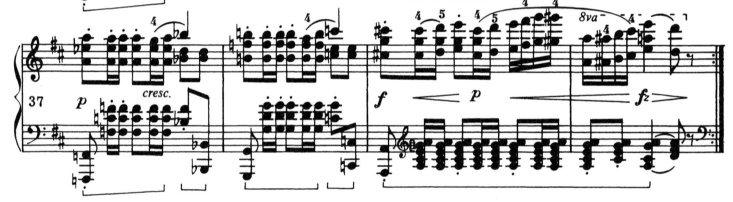

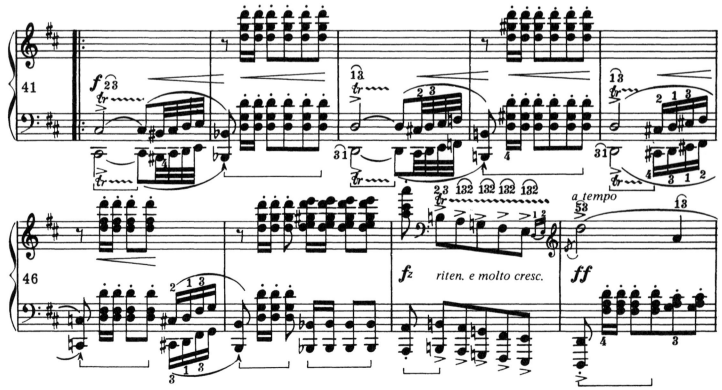

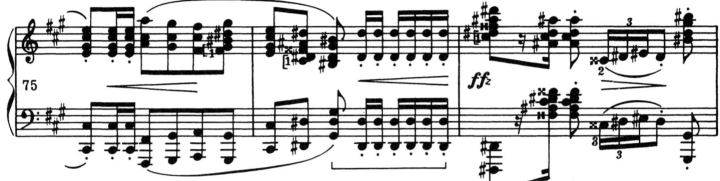

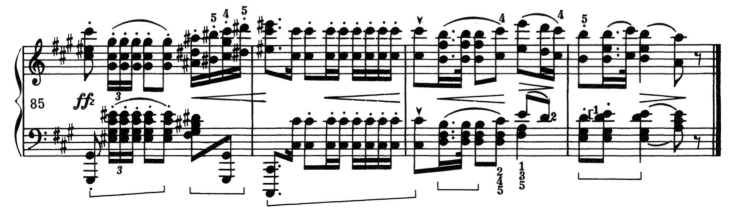

Fantaisie Impromptu
Op. 66

74

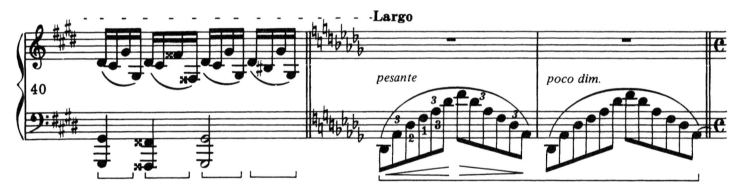

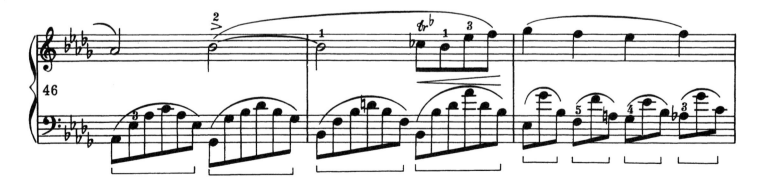

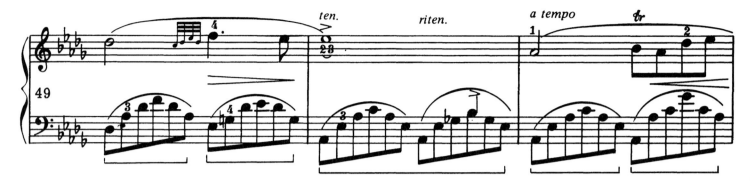

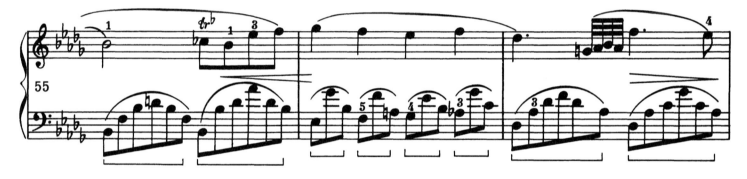

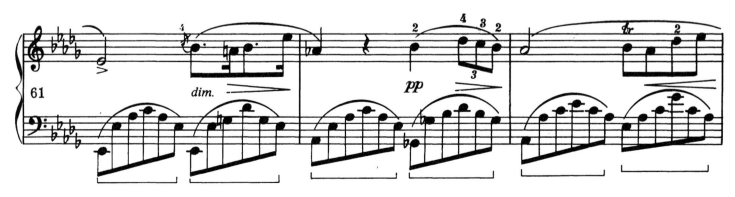

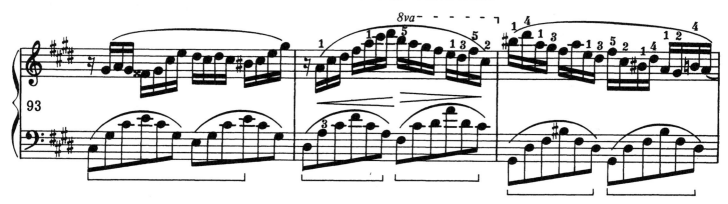

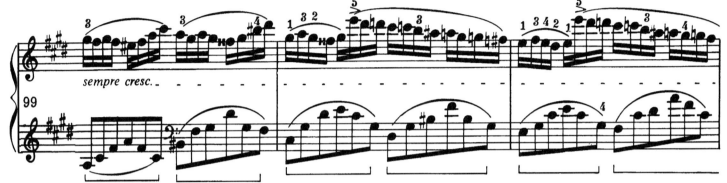

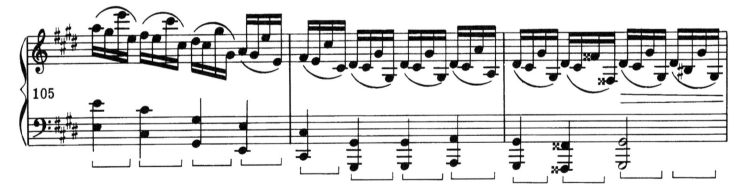

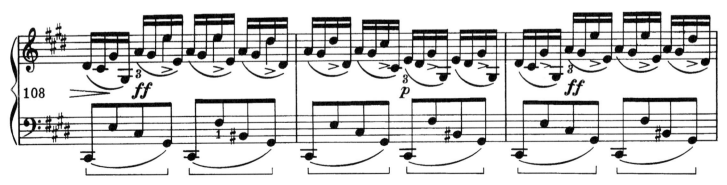

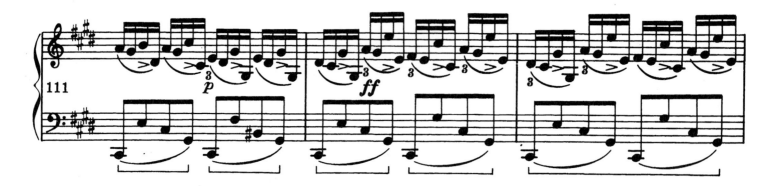

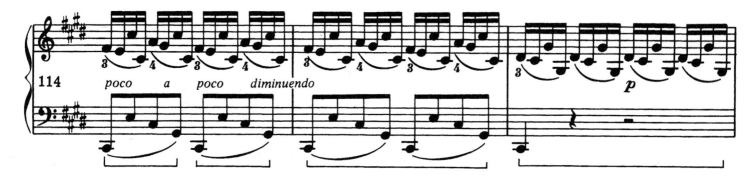

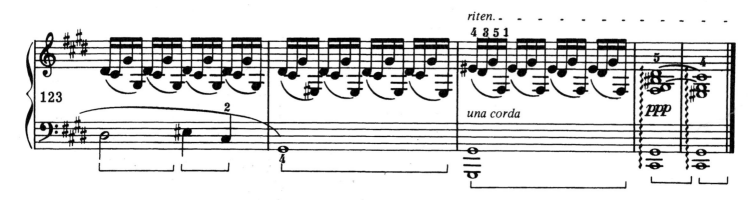